ART REVOLUTIONS
SURREALISM

Linda Bolton

PETER BEDRICK BOOKS

NTC/Contemporary Publishing Group

NEW YORK

This American edition published 2000 by Peter Bedrick Books,
a division of NTC/Contemporary Publishing Group, Inc.,
4255 West Touhy Avenue, Lincolnwood (Chicago),
Illinois 60646-1975 U.S.A.

First published in Great Britain in 2000 by Belitha Press Limited,
London House, Great Eastern Wharf, Parkgate Road, London SW11 4NQ

Editor Anna Claybourne
Designer Helen James
Picture Researcher Diana Morris
Educational Consultant Hester Collicutt
Consultants for US Edition Nathaniel Harris, Ruth Nason

Printed in China

International Standard Book Number: 0-87226-612-5

Library of Congress Cataloging-in-Publication data
is available from the United States Library of Congress.

00 01 02 03   15 14 13 12 11 10 9 8 7 6 5 4 3 2 1

Picture Credits:

Front cover: Joan Miró, The Harlequin's Carnival, 1924–25. © ADAGP Paris/DACS London 2000. Albright Knox Gallery, Buffalo. Photo Bridgeman Art Library. 1: René Magritte, The Listening Room, 1952. Kunsthaus Zürich, donated by Walter Haefner. Photo AKG London. 4: Hieronymus Bosch, The Garden of Earthly Delights, detail, 1505–10. Museo del Prado, Madrid. Photo AKG London. 5: Giuseppe Arcimboldo, Summer, 1563. Kunsthistorisches Museum, Vienna. Photo Bridgeman Art Library. 6: Giorgio de Chirico, The Song of Love, 1914. © SIAE Rome/DACS London 2000. Museum of Modern Art, New York. Nelson A. Rockefeller Bequest. Photo © 1999 MOMA, NY. 7t: Marc Chagall, Me and the Village, 1911. © ADAGP Paris/DACS London 2000. Museum of Modern Art, New York. Mrs. Simon Guggenheim Fund. Photo © 1999 MOMA, NY. 7b: René Magritte, Red Model, 1935. © ADAGP Paris/DACS London 2000. Musée National d'Art Moderne, Paris. Photo Peter Willi/Bridgeman Art Library. 8: Salvador Dalí, Slave Market with Disappearing Bust of Voltaire, 1940. © DEMART PRO ARTE, Paris & Geneva/DACS London 2000. Collection of The Salvador Dalí Museum, St. Petersburg, Florida. Photo © 1999 The Salvador Dalí Museum Inc. 9t: Salvador Dalí, Téléphone-Homard (Lobster Telephone), 1936. © DEMART PRO ARTE, Paris & Geneva/DACS London 2000. Photo Christie's Images/Superstock. 9b: Salvador Dalí, Metamorphosis of Narcissus, 1937. © DEMART PRO ARTE, Paris & Geneva/DACS London 2000. Tate Gallery, London. Photo John Webb/Tate Picture Library. 10: René Magritte, The Listening Room, 1952. Kunsthaus Zürich, donated by Walter Haefner. Photo AKG London. 11t: René Magritte, Not to be Reproduced, 1937. © ADAGP Paris/DACS London 2000. Museum Boijmans Van Beuningen, Rotterdam. 11b: Euclidean Walks, 1955. © ADAGP Paris/DACS London 2000. The William Hood Dunwoody Fund. Minneapolis Institute of Arts, Minnesota. Photo MIA. 12: Joan Miró, Person Throwing a Stone at a Bird, 1926. © ADAGP Paris/DACS London 2000. Museum of Modern Art, New York. Purchase. Photo © 1999 MOMA, NY. 13t: Joan Miró, The Harlequin's Carnival, 1924–25. © ADAGP Paris/DACS London 2000. Albright Knox Gallery, Buffalo. Photo Bridgeman Art Library. 13b: Joan Miró, Dog Barking at the Moon, 1926. © ADAGP Paris/ DACS London 2000. Philadelphia Museum of Art, A. E. Gallatin Collection. Photo PMA. 14: Max Ernst, At the First Clear Word, 1923. © ADAGP Paris/DACS London 2000. Kunstsammlung Nordrhein-Westfalen, Düsseldorf. Photo Peter Willi/ Bridgeman Art Library. 15: Max Ernst: Two Children Are Menaced by a Nightingale, 1924. © ADAGP Paris/DACS 2000 London. Museum of Modern Art, New York. Purchase. Photo © 1999 MOMA, NY. 16: Paul Delvaux, A Skeleton with Shell, 1944. © SABAM Brussels/ DACS London 2000. Private Collection. Photo © Foundation Paul Delvaux, St. Idesbald. 17: Paul Delvaux, A Mermaid in Full Moonlight, 1949. © SABAM Brussels/DACS London 2000. Southampton City Art Gallery. Photo Bridgeman Art Library. 18: Yves Tanguy, Days of Delay, 1937. © ARS New York/DACS London 2000. Musée National d'Art Moderne, Paris. Photo Philippe Migeat, Photothèque des collections du Mnam-cci. 19: Yves Tanguy, Mama, Papa Is Wounded, 1927. Museum of Modern Art, New York. Purchase. Photo © 1999 MOMA, NY. 20: Man Ray, Cadeau (The Gift), c. 1958, replica of 1921 original. © ADAGP Paris/DACS London 2000. Museum of Modern Art, New York. James Thrall Soby Fund. Photo © MOMA, NY. 21t: Man Ray, Les Larmes (Tears) c. 1932. © Man Ray Trust/ADAG Paris/DACS London 2000. Photo © Telimage, Paris – 1999. 21b: Man Ray, À l'Heure de l'Observatoire – les Amoureux (Observatory Time), 1932–34. Private Collection. © Man Ray Trust/ ADAGP Paris/DACS London 2000. Photo © Telimage, Paris 1999. 22: Francis Picabia, Feathers, 1921. © ADAGP Paris/DACS London 2000. Private Collection. Photo Giraudon. 23: Francis Picabia, The Handsome Pork Butcher, 1924–26 & 29–35. © ADAGP Paris/DACS London 2000. Tate Gallery, London. Photo Tate Picture Library. 24: Pierre Roy, A Naturalist's Study, 1928. © ADAGP Paris/DACS London 2000. Tate Gallery, London. Photo Tate Picture Library. 25: Pierre Roy, Danger on the Stairs, 1927–28. © ADAGP Paris/DACS London 2000. Museum of Modern Art, New York. Gift of Abby Aldrich Rockefeller. Photo © MOMA, NY. 26: Roland Penrose, Winged Domino – Portrait of Valentine Penrose, 1937. © Estate of Sir Roland Penrose. Private Collection. 27: Roland Penrose, Seeing Is Believing – The Invisible Isle, 1937. © Estate of Sir Roland Penrose. Private Collection. 28t: Meret Oppenheim, Lunch in Fur, 1936. © PRO LITERIS Zürich/DACS London 2000. Museum of Modern Art, New York. Purchase. Photo © MOMA, NY. 28b: Conroy Maddox, Passage de l'Opéra, 1940. © the artist. Tate Gallery, London. Photo Tate Picture Library. 29t: Leonora Carrington, Baby Giant, 1947. © ARS New York/DACS London 2000. Private Collection. Photo Bridgeman Art Library. 29b: Paul Nash, Harbor and Room, 1932–36. © The artist's estate. Tate Gallery, London. Photo Tate Picture Library.

CONTENTS

Useful words are explained on page 30.

SURREALIST DREAMS

Surrealism was an artistic and literary movement, at its height in the 1920s and 1930s. The Surrealists were in revolt against everyday reality and logic, and they aimed to shock and disturb people. Surrealist art is based on dreams and fantasies. It is filled with strange happenings and impossible meetings and mixings of images.

Surrealism began soon after World War I, which lasted from 1914 to 1918. Millions died during the war, and its horrors made many poets and artists feel that "progress," reason, and logic had failed. As early as 1916, a movement called Dada was poking fun at society and its ideas.

Surrealism was in some ways a continuation of Dada, but its outlook was more positive. In 1924, a French poet named André Breton founded the first Surrealist group in Paris. Breton said that artists should not copy reality, but should paint their dreams and imaginings.

Breton and his friends described their ideas as surreal. The word means "more than real." To Breton, dreams were mental realities. They were the secret driving force behind human actions – so they were more real than "real life." He wrote that "Surrealism is based on the belief in the superior reality of the dream."

Breton was soon joined by gifted poets and painters. Surrealism became an international movement, attracting artists from outside France. Most of them visited Paris and some settled there. Although they had similar ideas, Surrealist artists had different ways of working. Some painted scenes that were carefully composed, no matter how bizarre the content. Others practiced automatism – that is, they tried not to think about what they were writing or painting, putting down unforeseen words or images.

GIUSEPPE ARCIMBOLDO
Summer

1563, oil paint on canvas

The Surrealists also admired the work of Giuseppe Arcimboldo, a sixteenth-century Italian artist. He painted portraits made up of fruits and vegetables, such as this summery man. His nose is a zucchini, his lips are cherries, his teeth are a pea pod, and his cheek is a peach! Arcimboldo used one object to represent another. The Surrealists, too, often made pictures that can be seen in two ways.

HIERONYMUS BOSCH
The Garden of Earthly Delights

(Detail) 1505–10, oil paint and tempera on panel

Bosch was a Dutch artist who lived 500 years ago. He can be seen as a very early Surrealist. Instead of painting what he saw around him, he conjured up imaginary scenes of weird and fearful happenings. His works are nightmarish visions, full of giant birds, monstrous fish, and people trapped in transparent bubbles. The Surrealists admired Bosch's unique style, and were amazed that he had created these pictures so long ago.

Besides dreams, the Surrealists were interested in madness, memory, chance, and coincidence. They often put everyday objects in unexpected settings, and mixed very different ideas and images. For example, natural objects such as fruit and animals could be mixed with abstract shapes.

By the 1930s, the Surrealists were holding international exhibitions. They liked to play pranks and create scandals, so they became very well known. When France was invaded in World War II (1939–45), many Surrealists fled to the USA. After this, the movement faded away.

GIORGIO DE CHIRICO
The Song of Love

1914, oil paint on canvas

The Surrealists were strongly influenced by the Italian painter Giorgio de Chirico. This picture was painted by de Chirico some time before the Surrealist movement began, but, like Surrealist art, it is full of surprises and contradicts our ideas of reality. The title seems to have nothing to do with what is in the painting. Instead of lovers, we see a strange mixture of objects: a large rubber glove, a sculpted head, and a green ball. They are out of scale with one another and with the side of the house, whose wall is almost filled by the head and glove. To the left, a smokestack blows a puff of steam – or is it a floating cloud?

MARC CHAGALL
Me and the Village

1911, oil paint on canvas

Chagall was a Russian painter who lived mainly in Paris. This picture was inspired by Chagall's home town of Vitebsk in Russia. It is clearly not intended to be a realistic scene. A woman walks upside down, the large human face is green with white lips, and the sheep wears a string of beads. The houses and church are multi-colored and some of them are upside down. The picture is like a kaleidoscope of dreams and memories, thrown together and shaken up. Many Surrealists were inspired by Chagall. They often painted memories, and made people and objects defy gravity.

RENÉ MAGRITTE
Red Model

1935, oil paint on canvas

The title of this painting alerts us to the strangeness of the image at which we are looking. There is nothing red in this painting, and there is no model either – unless it is the two strange-looking objects in the foreground. These can be seen as either boots or feet, since the two things appear to have merged. The picture is typical of Magritte's work. It is traditional and realistic in the way in which it is painted, and the objects in it are quite ordinary. But this only makes the visual twist even more unsettling.

SALVADOR DALÍ   1904–1989

> *"The only difference between a madman and me is that I am not mad."*

The Spanish painter Salvador Dalí joined the Surrealists in 1929, after he moved from Spain to Paris and met André Breton. Dalí is the most famous Surrealist – even though Breton threw him out of the Surrealist movement for being too interested in making money!

Dali's pictures are carefully painted in traditional style, but show strange figures and objects in weird landscapes. He claimed that many of them were based on his own dreams. Dalí's personality was also surreal, though some people dismissed his antics as showmanship.

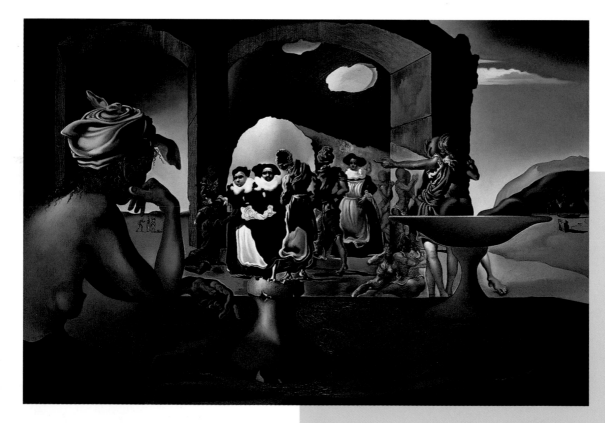

Slave Market with Disappearing Bust of Voltaire

1940, oil paint on canvas

Dalí was fascinated by the idea of seeing two different pictures in one painting. In the middle of this picture you can see either small figures in a marketplace, wearing black clothes from some past age, or a large head of a famous French writer, Voltaire (1694–1778). But, as with other visual tricks of this sort, you cannot see them both at once. Dalí gave this way of painting a typically extravagant title. He called it the "paranoiac-critical" method.

Lobster Telephone

1936, plastic, plaster, and mixed media

Dalí has replaced the handset of this telephone with a model lobster. In a strange way, the lobster, with its cylindrical body, curved tail, and pincers, is similar to a handset. But, at the same time, it is the last thing we expect to see on top of a telephone! It is both funny and disturbing to imagine picking up the lobster and holding it to your ear. Dalí's combination of two very different objects – one natural, one mechanical – is typical of the Surrealist way of creating unexpected effects.

Metamorphosis of Narcissus

1937, oil paint on canvas

In Greek myth, Narcissus was a beautiful boy who looked into a pool, fell in love with his own reflection, and died of longing. On the spot where he died, a flower grew, and it was named after him. Dalí's modern version of the story shows Narcissus and his reflection on the left, and also a strange stone hand holding an egg with the narcissus flower bursting out of it. This repeats the shape of the crouching figure of Narcissus. "Metamorphosis" means "transformation" – in this case into stone or into a flower.

SIGMUND FREUD (1856-1939)

The Surrealists were influenced by Freud's ideas. He claimed that unconscious motives directed many human actions. People thought they knew why they did things, but the true reasons were sometimes hidden in the unconscious mind.

RENÉ MAGRITTE 1898–1967

Magritte was a Belgian artist. He met the Surrealists when he spent three years in Paris, from 1927 to 1930. His strange, puzzling paintings may remind you of dreams – even nightmares. Yet they are also very clear and beautiful, with calm, simple colors and shapes.

Magritte had several favorite subjects which appear over and again in his work – such as steam trains and men in derbies. He often used words in his paintings, and made familiar objects seem strange by changing their scale or putting them in impossible settings.

The Listening Room

1952, oil paint
on canvas

This giant apple fills an otherwise empty room, like something from *Alice in Wonderland*. In a way, the fruit's immense presence is threatening, and the title, *The Listening Room*, makes you feel that something is about to happen. The most obvious fact about the scene is that the apple is too large to have been put in the room through its door or window. Of course, a Surrealist might think in terms of building the house around the apple! Magritte plays with words and objects in his paintings, using a few simple elements to make powerful, striking images.

Not to be Reproduced

1937, oil paint on canvas

Magritte gave this eerie painting a clever title. "Not to be reproduced" is a phrase often used by artists who do not want their work to be copied. At the same time, the title makes you think about what is happening in the painting. The mirror does not reflect the man's face, as you would expect. Instead, it "reproduces" his back – and yet it reflects the book on the shelf normally! Although we cannot see his face, this is a portrait of Edward James, an English collector of Surrealist objects. He owned Dalí's famous *Lobster Telephone* (page 9) and Magritte's *Red Model* (page 7).

Euclidean Walks

1955, oil paint on canvas

CHANGE OF SCALE

One of Magritte's visual tricks was to put objects together but change the normal relationship between their sizes. So he painted a room-sized apple, a train steaming out of a fireplace, and a bedroom with a glass and comb as big as a closet.

Many of Magritte's works are paintings that include other paintings. Here, a picture rests on an easel in front of a window. The painting fits so perfectly into the scene behind it that it is easy to believe that the painting is an identical copy of the real scene – but that might not be true at all. Magritte pulls off another visual trick by putting two almost identical cones in the painting, but while one is a spire on top of a tower, the other is a road disappearing into the distance. Perhaps the title gives us a clue. Euclid was the inventor of geometry, the science of shapes.

JOAN MIRÓ 1893–1983

"The most Surrealist of us all."

Like Dalí, Miró was born in Spain, but he spent most of his working life in Paris. He was often reduced to poverty, and sometimes had hardly anything to eat. Miró said that hunger made him hallucinate. As a result, he saw all sorts of strange visions, and copied them in his work.

Like other Surrealists, Miró was fascinated by childhood. Many Surrealists believed that children, unlike adults, saw things purely and vividly. Miró wanted to be like a child when he painted. He tried to free his unconscious mind and let his emotions and imagination take over.

Person Throwing a Stone at a Bird

1926, oil paint on canvas

You can see Miró's childlike style in this colorful scene, with its yellow sand, black sea, and green sky. There is an odd-looking figure with a giant foot and a single eye – the title tells us this is a person. Miró's bird is made of bright, mostly geometric shapes, and the stone's flight is marked with a dotted line. Strangest of all, the stone-thrower seems to have no arms to throw with!

The Harlequin's Carnival

1924–25, oil paint on canvas

The atmosphere inside this room is that of a party, where fantastic creatures and shapes leap about and play with one another. The musical notes on the wall suggest that the room is full of lively sounds to which the figures are dancing. They seem to be bouncing on coils, jumping from the ladder, and swimming through the air. The night sky, seen through the window on the right, looks peaceful when compared with the wild scene inside.

AUTOMATISM

Surrealists wanted to free the unconscious mind. One way was to go into a sort of trance, letting the hand draw or write automatically. A famous American painter, Jackson Pollock, was influenced by the idea.

Dog Barking at the Moon

1926, oil paint on canvas

The dog and the moon in this painting look a little like cartoons – strangely distorted and colorful. At the same time, the dark sky and the ladder reaching into nothingness give the picture a feeling of sadness. This may be because Miró's father died the year it was painted. Like many of Miró's pictures, this one was given its title by his friends, after it was finished.

MAX ERNST

1891–1976

"I saw myself falling in love with what I saw."

Max Ernst was born in Germany. He became a leader of the Dada movement before joining the Surrealists in Paris. Some of his most original works exploited accidental effects. This first happened one rainy day when Ernst was staying at a seaside inn, and began to stare at the floor.

Fascinated by what he saw, Ernst started to make rubbings of the floorboards. Moving the paper at random, he created images of strange visions and other worlds. He also experimented by rubbing paper on tree bark, drawing with candle smoke, and smudging blobs of paint.

At the First Clear Word

1923, oil paint on plaster, transferred to canvas

Besides creating experimental works, Ernst also followed the Surrealist practice of painting clear, bright pictures with mysterious subjects. Here, a hand pokes through a windowlike hole to hold a ball that dangles from a piece of string. The simple geometrical shapes are combined with natural elements – two plants and a green insect, which is attached to the string and ball. The meaning of the painting, and its connection with the title, are difficult – probably impossible – to establish. Ernst himself may not have known the answer if he was painting without a conscious plan. He has provided the images. We are free to interpret them as we choose.

2 enfants sont menacés par un rossignol /M. ernst

Two Children Are Menaced by a Nightingale

1924, oil paint on canvas with wood

The nightingale is known for its sweet singing, not for scaring children! And there are more than two figures here – one girl is running, a second lies on the grass, and a third is held by a man on the roof. The tiny nightingale flutters quietly on the left of the picture.

Ernst has written the mysterious title of this painting on the frame. And some parts of the picture – the gate and the strange red buzzer high on the right – are made of wood and stuck to the frame. It is as if they offer an escape out of the painting and into a three-dimensional world. Ernst's picture makes us think of being trapped in a strange hallucination, or perhaps a nightmare.

PAUL DELVAUX 1897–1994

"I thought only of trying to express something which was quite indefinable."

Delvaux was born in Belgium and trained as a painter, but only became a Surrealist in the 1930s. He was inspired by the work of de Chirico, whom he called "the poet of emptiness." Delvaux wanted to create the same kind of art.

He admired de Chirico's simple, poetic style and his use of shadows. His paintings also use many images favored by de Chirico, such as Greek temples and steam trains. Delvaux remained a Surrealist painter for the rest of his very long life.

A Skeleton with Shell

1944, oil paint on masonite

Delvaux often used classical scenes in his paintings. Here, two skeletons are inside what seems to be an ancient Greek temple, with a ring of tall stone columns around them and an ornate dome above. The strangeness of this picture comes partly from the fact that, instead of lying dead and unmoving, the skeletons are behaving like living people. One stoops to pick up a shell from the tiled floor, and the other sits up in a sofalike seat called a chaise longue. In the far distance, a train approaches. Its presence among the columns and statues in the background confirms that ordinary time has no meaning here.

A Mermaid in Full Moonlight

1949, oil paint on wood

A mermaid belongs in the sea. How did she reach this cold, deserted classical square? The fact that she is on a plinth or base suggests that she might be a statue, but she seems to be very much alive. As in so many Surrealist pictures, something natural – or, in this case, supernatural – is set against the solid geometric shapes of the city. Look at the time on the clock tower – a quarter past twelve. It is the "witching hour" – the hour between midnight and one o'clock. According to fairy tales, this is when humans sleep and mythical dream creatures inhabit the world. The everyday is turned into the magical and strange. Perhaps, by daybreak, the mermaid will have turned to stone. Delvaux was very clearly inspired by dreams. Most of his pictures are night scenes with beautiful, mysterious women.

YVES TANGUY

1900–1955

"Painter of subterranean and oceanic marvels."

Yves Tanguy (pronounced "tong-ee") was born in Paris, and had several jobs. As a merchant seaman, he went to South America and Africa. He also worked in a news clippings agency, as a tram driver, and as a grilled-sandwich maker. Then, one day, from a bus, he saw a painting by de Chirico in the window of an art gallery.

He began to paint, became a close friend of André Breton, and joined the Surrealists. His paintings do not show recognizable objects or scenes. Instead, they are full of strange jellylike shapes, crawling on moonlike surfaces. This may reflect Tanguy's fascination with the curious rock formations he saw during a trip to Africa.

Days of Delay

1937, oil paint on canvas

The title *Days of Delay* adds to the strangeness of this painting, in which unfamiliar shapes seem to crawl across a smooth, empty landscape. The top part of the painting could represent the sky or it could be the land sweeping upward to fill the whole painting. The place could be the desert, the moon, or another planet. Although this looks like a space-age vision, it could not have been based on a real moon-scape. It was created long before the first moon landing in 1969.

YVES TANGUY. 17

Mama, Papa Is Wounded!

1927, oil paint
on canvas

The alarming title of
this painting makes
us expect an eventful
or even tragic scene,
and so we may look
for injured people or
dangerous objects.
But all we can see
are strange scattered
shapes. What is the prickly stem on the right?
What is the streaked black cloud around its
top? And what are the white lines joining the
objects on the left? Tanguy does not suggest
any explanation. He has let his unconscious
mind produce a picture that the viewer must
respond to emotionally. Looking at Tanguy's
pictures is a little like waking up from a
disturbing dream. We struggle to work out
the meaning of the things we have seen.

MENTAL LANDSCAPE

Tanguy and Dalí both painted
smooth, barren landscapes that
stretched far into the distance,
ending in a high horizon.
Exaggerated distances are a
common feature of dreams.

MAN RAY

1890–1976

Man Ray was an American photographer who became part of the Surrealist movement in Paris. He used many different materials, or media, in his art. He produced Surrealist paintings and objects, but is most famous for his photographs.

Ray was very successful as a fashion and portrait photographer. But he believed that photography did not have to be realistic – it could be used for all sorts of artistic purposes. He made abstract and surreal images that have become famous.

The Gift

1958 (replica of original of 1921), painted flatiron and tacks

Man Ray made this sculpture by sticking a row of sharp tacks onto a household iron. Instead of being a helpful domestic device, the iron is now useless – even dangerous. Looking at it makes you think of what would happen if you tried to iron something with it. The title may once have seemed to be a joke, but now anyone would like to receive an important Surrealist work as a gift! Combining two everyday things – with two different uses – creates something that is funny, shocking, and unnerving, all at the same time. Artworks that use manufactured objects in this way are sometimes known as ready-mades.

Glass Tears

1930–33, silver print

This is one of Man Ray's most famous photos. It shows part of a woman's face in close-up. We can see clearly the round, shiny glass tears stuck onto her cheeks, and her long false eyelashes. Her stage make-up and exaggerated expression make her look like an actress in a silent movie. This is not intended to convince us that the woman is crying. Instead, Man Ray has focused on the forms of the artificial tears and lashes and wide oval eyes. The shapes look almost like parts of an abstract painting.

PHOTO NOVELTIES

Man Ray created new artistic effects by using photographic techniques. One was solarization, in which the light and dark tones of the image were reversed, so that it appeared to be surrounded by sunglow. Another type of photo, the Rayograph, was like abstract art. It was made by placing objects directly on photo paper and exposing it to the light.

Observatory Time

1932–34, oil paint on canvas

Man Ray wrote the following words about this surreal image: "The red lips floated in a bluish sky over a twilit landscape, with an observatory ... dimly indicated on the horizon." He said the lips were so large that they looked like two bodies – "like the earth and sky, like you and me." Man Ray makes the scene sound peaceful, but it is also scary and strange, with the huge pair of lips hovering like a menacing UFO.

FRANCIS PICABIA 1878–1953

"The paintings that I make are very much in rapport with my life."

Picabia was born in Paris. During his lifetime he used many different artistic styles. He worked as a Cubist with artists such as Picasso, and then became part of the zany Dada movement, which developed in Switzerland and spread to Europe and the United States.

The Dadaists created deliberately shocking works. They liked accidental effects and nonsensical images. The movement ended in 1922, but the Surrealists adopted many of the same ideas, and Picabia joined them. He was famous for his cover designs for *Littérature*, a Surrealist magazine.

Feathers

1921, oil paint and collage

Here Picabia has used feathers, pasta, paper, and other items to create a picture of a beach. The feathers represent palm fronds and the sticks of pasta look like steps up the side of a sand dune. In the green area, corn plasters have been stuck on to represent pebbles. Instead of using a canvas as the base for his work, Picabia has used what looks like a wooden tray. Collage is a way of creating images of two things at once (for example, feathers and palm fronds) – which we have seen, for instance from the example of Dalí, to be a feature of Surrealist works.

Francis Picabia

The Handsome Pork Butcher

1935, oil paint
on canvas

Picabia painted this strange portrait on top of another of his works – a collage which he had completed a few years earlier. You can see the shapes of a man's eyes and mustache, his pink face, and his hair made out of real plastic combs. But on top of this Picabia has painted what looks like the outline of a woman's face. When we have been looking for a while, the images become more, not less, confused. They start to flick backward and forward, as in an optical illusion. The identity of the person or persons in the picture becomes more and more doubtful – perhaps they are just aspects of the same person.

DECALCOMANIA

In this Surrealist technique, patches of color are dabbed on a sheet of paper. While it is still wet, a second sheet is put over it, moved gently, and then peeled away. The resulting image can be left as it is or worked on further by the artist.

PIERRE ROY

1880–1950

"Surprises in daylight."

Pierre Roy began his career working in an architect's office, but joined the Surrealist movement after meeting Giorgio de Chirico (see page 6) in Paris. He was greatly impressed by de Chirico, whom he called the father of Surrealism.

Roy's own pictures, like those of de Chirico and Magritte, look realistic but put objects in unlikely combinations to produce dreamlike scenes. Roy claimed he often worked out the meanings of his paintings months after they were finished.

A Naturalist's Study

1928, oil paint on canvas

Roy often painted snakes, and in this picture a snakelike shape seems to be pinned to the floor. This snake and the string of eggs hanging on the wall might belong to a naturalist – someone who studies nature and wildlife. But what about the wheel and the train? As in many Surrealist works, natural and mechanical images are mixed together. And, like Magritte and Dalí, Roy plays with double possibilities. Are we looking at the train through a window, or is it part of a picture on the wall? At what point does the steam from the train turn into clouds? The Surrealists loved such mysteries.

Danger on the Stairs

1927–28, oil paint on canvas

The danger on these stairs is very clear. The snake is frightening because it is not in the surroundings we would expect – a zoo or the jungle. Instead, it is making its way downstairs, past the closed doors of someone's Paris apartment and along the polished hall. Roy plays on our fears by bringing something wild and dangerous into a safe, everyday setting. Yet, at the same time, these two opposed elements are artistically related – the snake's writhing form is echoed in the twisting spiral of the staircase and banisters.

STRANGE SIGHTS

Roy, Dalí, and Magritte painted in a smooth, carefully finished "academic" style, often regarded as old-fashioned. But their realistic technique actually gave their compositions added shock value.

ROLAND PENROSE

"Writing tomorrow's news in the sky."

Roland Penrose was born in London and went to Paris after World War I, to study art. He was introduced to Surrealism by Max Ernst (see pages 14–15) and they became good friends. Later, Penrose introduced Surrealism to Britain.

Besides being a painter and sculptor, Penrose used his money to promote art and fund artists. He organized a big Surrealist exhibition in London in 1936, and wrote several books, including one about the great twentieth-century artist Picasso.

Winged Domino – Portrait of Valentine

1937, oil paint on canvas

The second part of the title of this painting tells us it is a portrait, in fact of the artist's wife. But something else is going on here too. The very features which help us recognize a person are covered up by butterflies. A domino is a type of mask, and, although she does not seem to be wearing a mask, Valentine's blue skin makes her look strange and unnatural. With her calm, cold stillness, her thorny necklace, and the bird in her hair, she looks like a statue overrun by wildlife.

Seeing Is Believing – The Invisible Isle

1937, oil paint on canvas

The isle mentioned in the title of this painting is formed where a cascade of hair meets an array of buildinglike shapes and a hand rising out of a shining sea. There is little natural landscape to be seen, but the image of an island is created from the other elements. Next to the clearly shown left hand there is what looks like a right hand, seen as a kind of ghostly negative. You should try looking at this picture upside down. As a Surrealist painting, it works just as well!

SURREALIST SHOWTIME

At Penrose's 1936 exhibition in London, to give a talk about plunging into the unconscious mind, Dalí wore a diving suit. But he forgot to attach an air tube, and his helmet stuck. He almost suffocated before it was pried off with a pool cue!

MORE SURREALISM

The Surrealist movement inspired many artists to try its methods and media. On these two pages are just a few of the artworks they created.

These works contain several of the objects and ideas mentioned earlier in the book, such as men in derbies and things that seem out of place.

MERET OPPENHEIM
Lunch in Fur

1936, fur-covered cup, saucer, and spoon

Oppenheim (1913–85) was a Berlin-born painter and object-maker. Her fur-covered cup and saucer have become one of the most memorable Surrealist images.

CONROY MADDOX
Passage de l'Opéra

1940, oil paint on canvas

Maddox (born 1912) is a British Surrealist artist whose work looks similar to that of Magritte (pages 10–11). Neat-looking men in coats and derby hats stroll along, but the startling lion in the foreground makes this scene far from normal. Its whiteness makes it look like a statue – but its expression and paw-held cloak make it seem alive and menacing.

LEONORA CARRINGTON
Baby Giant

1947, oil paint on canvas

Carrington was born in Britain in 1917, but settled in Mexico. In this picture the giant baby, holding an egg, towers over two worlds – a seascape with whales and Viking ships, and a woodland with magical creatures. Birds fly out of the figure's cloak and flap around her.

PAUL NASH
Harbor and Room

1932–36, oil paint on canvas

Nash (1889–1946) was another British Surrealist whose work resembles that of Magritte and Delvaux. The scene in this painting is both the inside of a room, and, on a completely different scale, a harbor. Water comes into the room and washes across the tiled floor at an angle.

abstract art Art that does not show images from the real world or even fantasies. It relies on shape, texture, and color to interest the viewer.

bust A statue of a head and shoulders.

canvas A strong fabric on which artists paint.

classical A word used to describe anything to do with the ancient Greeks and Romans.

collage A collection of materials, such as paper, fabric, and photos, stuck onto a background.

Cubism An art movement in which artists made paintings and collages using geometric shapes such as cubes, cylinders, and cones.

geometry The part of math that deals with lines, shapes, and surfaces. Many Surrealist pictures include geometric images such as spheres, curves, and dotted lines.

hallucination An image of something that is not really there, but is produced by your brain. Drugs can make people hallucinate, and so can being very hungry, tired, or ill.

image A picture or idea.

masonite A kind of tough board made from wood fiber, used by some artists to paint on.

media The types of paint and materials an artist uses to make a work of art.

movement A style or period of art, usually created when a group of artists get together.

optical illusion A picture that plays tricks on your eyes and brain – such as Dalí's paranoiac-critical paintings.

paranoiac-critical method A phrase invented by Dalí to describe pictures that can be seen in two completely different ways.

plinth The base on which a statue rests.

reality The real things that surround us, such as houses and people, as opposed to what we see in dreams and in our imagination.

replica An exact copy of something.

surreal More than real, or "on top of" real. This word is made up of *sur* (the French word for "on") and the word "real."

tempera A type of paint made of colored powder mixed with egg white.

unconscious A part of your mind that you do not use for thinking. You are not aware of your unconscious mind, but it can have an effect on your dreams and fears. In their work, the Surrealists tried to let their unconscious minds take over from rational thought.

vision Something that we can see in our imagination or in a hallucination.

SURREALIST TIMES

1900 Sigmund Freud publishes *The Interpretation of Dreams*, a book about the unconscious mind.

1921 André Breton visits Freud in Vienna.

1924 Breton publishes the first *Surrealist Manifesto*, explaining what the Surrealists are trying to do. *The Surrealist Revolution*, the first Surrealist magazine, is published.

1925 First Surrealist exhibition takes place in Galerie Pierre, Paris.

1926 Man Ray makes Surrealist film, *Emak Bakia*. Belgian Surrealist group is started.

1928 Breton publishes book *Surrealism and Painting*. Dalí and his friend Luis Buñuel make a Surrealist movie, *Un Chien Andalou*.

1930 Breton publishes second *Surrealist Manifesto*. A magazine is started called *Surrealism in the Service of the Revolution*.

1933 Start of Surrealist magazine *Minotaur*.

1935 International Surrealist exhibition is shown in Copenhagen and Tenerife. First *International Bulletin of Surrealism* is published in Prague.

1936 An exhibition of Surrealist objects takes place at Galerie Ratton, Paris. An international Surrealist exhibition is shown in London. The Museum of Modern Art, New York, stages the exhibition *Fantastic Art: Dada and Surrealism*.

1938 International Surrealist exhibitions take place in Paris and Amsterdam.

FURTHER INFORMATION

Museums to visit

Surrealist art can be seen in museums and art galleries all over the world. Some of the biggest collections are in the United States, including the **Salvador Dalí Museum**, St. Petersburg, Florida, and the **Museum of Modern Art**, New York.

In Europe you can visit the **Dalí Museum**, Figueras, Spain, and the **Fundacio Joan Miró**, Palma, Majorca, Balearic Islands, Spain. The **Musée Royaux des Beaux-Arts**, Brussels (for Magritte and Delvaux), and the **Paul Delvaux Museum**, Saint Idesbald, are two collections in Belgium.

In the UK, the **Tate Modern**, London, and the **Brighton Art Museum**, both house many interesting examples of Surrealist art.

Websites to browse

http://www.surrealist.com/index.html
http://www.duke.edu/web//lit132/index.html
http://www.surrealism.co.uk

Books to Read

Dalí's Mustache by Salvador Dalí and Philippe Halsman, Abbeville, 1994

Hello Fruit Face! The Pictures of Guiseppe Arcimboldo by Claudia Strand, from the *Adventures in Art* series, Prestel, 1999

Marc Chagall: Life is a Dream by Brigitta Höppler, from the *Adventures in Art* series, Prestel, 1998

Miró in his Studio by Joan Punyet Miró, Thames & Hudson, London, 1996

Now You See It – Now You Don't: René Magritte by Angela Wenzel, from the *Adventures in Art* series, Prestel, 1998

Salvador Dalí by Mike Venezia, from the *Getting to Know the World's Greatest Artists* series, Children's Press, 1994

The Essential Salvador Dalí by Robert Goff, Andrews McMeel, 1998

INDEX